Kirsty O'Donnell is an associate within the serious injury team at Digby Brown LLP. Digby Brown LLP are ranked in Chambers UK 2021 as band 1 for personal injury. Kirsty is part of the team who won the prestigious Catastrophic Injury Team of the Year Award at the UK wide Personal Injury Awards 2020 and litigation team of the year at the Scottish Legal Awards 2021. She is an accredited specialist in personal injury by the Law Society of Scotland and is accredited as a senior litigator by the Association of Personal Injury Lawyers (APIL). Kirsty is also a tutor on the diploma in legal practice post graduate course at the University of Glasgow for civil litigation.

Kirsty specialises in traumatic brain injury, spinal cord injury and amputation cases and also has significant experience in acting for families of individuals killed as a result of accidents. She acts for those injured in different types of accidents including workplace, road traffic, occupier's liability and public liability cases. She also has significant advocacy experience in the Sheriff Courts, ASPIC and the Court of Session in Scotland.

A Practical Guide to Periodical Payment Orders in Personal Injury Cases in Scotland

A Practical Guide to Periodical Payment Orders in Personal Injury Cases in Scotland

Kirsty O'Donnell LLB (Hons) Dip. L.P
Associate Solicitor, Digby Brown LLP

Law Brief Publishing

Published 2021 by Law Brief Publishing, an imprint of Law Brief Publishing Ltd
30 The Parks
Minehead
Somerset
TA24 8BT

www.lawbriefpublishing.com

Paperback: 978-1-914608-15-5

PREFACE

The purpose of this book is to provide an introduction to periodical payment orders for solicitors working in the personal injury field. The main aims are: (i) to highlight the circumstances where a periodical payment order might be advantageous to an injured party and when it may not be, (ii) to highlight the practicalities surrounding them and their application and (iii) to highlight the need to consider periodical payment orders appropriate cases when the Damages (Investment Returns and Periodical Payments) (Scotland) Act 2019 comes into force. It is not however anticipated that, when this legislation is enacted, it will result in the flood gates opening. The majority of cases will still settle by means of a traditional lump sum award but consideration of this mode of settlement is required in serious injury cases.

I wish to extend my grateful thanks to my colleagues in this specialist field who kindly agreed to share their wealth of experience and knowledge with me when I was writing this textbook. John Pollock, consulting actuary at Pollock and Galbraith, Mark Traynor, law accountant at Alex Quinn & Partners and Chris Stewart, head of the serious injury team at Digby Brown LLP all generously agreed to review this textbook from a technical perspective and I am very grateful for their comments and suggestions.

The law was believed to be accurate as at 1 October 2021.

Kirsty O'Donnell
October 2021

CONTENTS

CHAPTER ONE

INTRODUCTION

It is a long-established principle in personal injury cases that the objective is for the injured party to secure full compensation as a result of the claim process. This is otherwise known as the 100% compensation principle (see *Wells v Wells [1999] 1 AC 345*). This principle was then re-iterated in *Simon v Helmot [2012] UKPC 5*:

> "*The only principle of law is that the claimant should receive full compensation for the loss which he has suffered as a result of the defendant's tort, not a penny more but not a penny less.*"

The limitations of assessing damages as a lump sum award and the guess work that was associated with calculating future losses were however highlighted in *Wells* and it was suggested that a straightforward solution, even at that time, was to give the court the power to award periodical payments.

In serious injury cases and indeed any case with future pecuniary losses, practitioners must be alive to the manner in which full compensation can be achieved on a practical level. In Scotland, the methodology behind this at present is for a lump sum to be awarded to the pursuer, which is discounted to take into account various contingencies and to negate the expected investment return through the application of the discount rate (applicable at the date of settlement). At the time of writing in 2021, this is set at -0.75% in Scotland. However, for over 15 years, the discount rate was 2.5%, which led to many pursuers being under-compensated due to the manner in which lump sum awards required to be calculated. In effect, the discount rate is the 'real return.' The pursuer is expected to earn a return of -0.75% relative to the assumed growth in the head of claim

The aim of this book is to provide practical advice and considerations for any personal injury lawyer looking to explore settlement of a case by means of a periodical payment order. The two main risks that periodical payment orders remove from the calculation of a traditional lump sum are (i) longevity and (ii) investment risk. These will be discussed more fully later in the book. This book will examine the pros and cons of where a periodical payment order may be appropriate however, there are some situations, such as where the level of contributory negligence will be high, where a periodical payment order will not be suitable or workable to meet the pursuer's needs.

This is new territory in Scotland and it is anticipated that the approach taken in other UK jurisdictions will be considered as solicitors and the courts find their way in determining their application in Scotland. These types of orders generally will however relate to cases of more substantial value. The key take away is that practitioners will be required to consider and provide advice on this mode of settlement once the rules come into force but there is nothing precluding their use at present if both parties agree to disposing of the case by means of a periodical payment order.

This is not to say that a lump sum award is no longer the best way of settling serious injury cases and that periodical payment orders are the future. This decision will be case-dependent and every case will turn on their facts. A number of factors must be taken into account in a balancing exercise when coming to the decision relating to their use after obtaining the appropriate expert input, the views of the client and looking at the case as a whole. At the end of the day, it is a matter for the client but the added layer here is that if you proceed to court when part 2 of the Act is in force, there is a risk that a periodical payment order is imposed, even if it is against your client's wishes, if the court considers that this will best suit the needs of the injured party. It should however be noted that the court will always have special regard to the pursuer's needs and preferences when doing so in terms of the legislation.

PART I

LEGISLATION

CHAPTER TWO

THE DAMAGES (INVESTMENT RETURNS AND PERIODICAL PAYMENTS (SCOTLAND) ACT 2019

One of the purposes of The Damages (Investment Returns and Periodical Payments) (Scotland) Act 2019 ("the Act") was to ensure that injured parties claiming for compensation achieved a fair settlement, particularly when future loss claims were incorporated into their claim. It was identified that there was a real need for the calculation of these future losses to be carried out in a fair and transparent manner. It is no secret that the calculation of awards in serious injury cases on a multiplier/multiplicand basis has its deficiencies. The bill for the Act was passed by the Scottish Parliament on 19 March 2019 and received royal assent on 24 April 2019. It was then enacted in part on 1 July 2019.

Part 1 of the Act deals with the return on investment of damages and the discount rate. Periodical payment orders are dealt with in part 2.

Section 3 of the Act amends section 2 of the Damages Act 1996 as follows:

"(1) In section 2 of the Damages Act 1996—

(a) after subsection (A1) there is inserted—

(A2) A court awarding damages for future pecuniary loss in respect of personal injury—

(a) must—

(i) consider whether to make an order under which those damages wholly or partly take the form of periodical payments, and

(ii) have special regard to the pursuer's needs and preferences when doing so, and

(b) may make such an order with or without the consent of the parties.",

(b) in subsection (1), for the words "in an action for personal injury" there is substituted "in respect of personal injury (other than damages for future pecuniary loss)"

(c) after subsection (1) there is inserted—

"(1A) A court may not make an order for periodical payments unless it is satisfied that the continuity of payment under the order is reasonably secure.

(1B) When a court makes an order for periodical payments, it must state why it is satisfied that the continuity of payment under the order is reasonably secure.",

the title of the section becomes "Periodical payment orders".

Once this part of the legislation is in force, there will be a requirement for the court to consider the use of periodical payment orders in all cases where future pecuniary loss claims are awarded. It is important to note that this can be with or without the consent of the parties to the action if the court considers it the best vehicle for settlement when considering the injured party's needs. Detailed advice therefore will require to be provided to clients proceeding to Court of this potential outcome and a note of that advice recorded and retained on file.

The legislation goes on to highlight the need for the future periodical payments to be "reasonably secure" and further provisions set out the requirements for this in section 2 of the Act. There is an obvious need for practitioners to satisfy themselves and the court that the compensator can be reasonably considered to be able to continue to make payments until the injured party's death otherwise practitioners would be deemed negligent.

Section 2 of the Act also makes provision for index linking of payments to ensure that payments in the future reflect "real money" terms and this will be discussed in more detail later in this book. It is important that this is not neglected in the agreement itself to ensure that the value of the periodical payment in 40 years for argument's sake, is not less than it should be due to inflation/change in salaries. This aspect of the periodical payments calculation will require specialist input from expert advisors to ensure that appropriate calculations are used when referring to periodical payments in the periodical payment order agreement itself.

Section 4 of the Act regulates the variation or suspension of the periodical payment order, which again will be discussed more fully later. It is important to note that ultimately, in the vast majority of cases where a periodical payment order is agreed between parties (as opposed to being imposed by court) that the finer points of the agreement will be subject to negotiation. If parties do however require a provision for variation or suspension of the annual payments, then this must be specifically included in the agreement. It is not something that can be applied for at a later date if the pursuer's situation changes.

In practice, even when the broad terms of a periodical payment order are agreed between parties, the second stage of actually formalising the terms of the agreement itself is often a hard-fought negotiation. It is important that the agreement also accurately reflects what you want it to say from a technical point of view. This seems obvious but it is imperative that it is checked properly as practitioners ordinarily do not have the skill set to check complex financial calculations and equations. This will be covered later but input from expert advisors is required to check formulae for the future calculations, particularly if there are variations to the payment calculations in the future to reflect an injured party's individual needs. Even simple points such as the date when payments are made or payments calculated can be important in the calculation itself to ensure the latest updated index is used and in turn the annual payment is calculated correctly.

The rules of court regulating this legislation are awaited and it remains to be seen what additional duties will be placed on practitioners by the court over and above the terms of the Act. It is hoped that these rules will be in force in the near future to allow for clearer advice to be given to injured parties regarding the applicability of periodical payment orders, rather than simply being an option if both parties agree to them (and the terms of the agreement thereafter being acceptable to both parties). As mutual consent is required, at the moment, it simply is not possible to settle the case in this manner if only one party wants it so.

CHAPTER THREE

100% COMPENSATION PRINCIPLE

There are a number of factors, including often a vast array of expert reports, that require to be balanced when achieving fair compensation for an injured party. It is a well-established principle of law that an award of damages, insofar as possible, is intended to put the injured party in the position they would have been had they not been injured for both pecuniary and non-pecuniary losses. This principle is, of course, underpinned by the concept of reasonableness, which is determined by the specific needs for the individual injured party.

In *Heil v Rankin and associated appeals [2000] 2 W.L.R 1173*, Lord Woolf stated:

> *"The aim of an award of damages for personal injury is to provide compensation. The principle is that 'full compensation' should be provided. ... This principle of full compensation applies to pecuniary and non-pecuniary damage alike. ... Compensation must remain fair, reasonable and just. Fair compensation for the injured person. The level must also not result in injustice to the defendant, and it must not be out of accord with what society as a whole would perceive as reasonable".*

Serious injury cases are usually quite unique and although broadly similar issues arise, the cases themselves are individual in nature and advice requires to be tailored to fit specific needs of the client. Sadly, these individuals are often faced with expert evidence suggesting that their life expectancy is reduced as a result of their injuries sustained at the time of the accident. Ultimately, if a case cannot be resolved extra-judicially, this will be a matter for the court to decide upon but as you will be aware, life expectancy is often a hotly disputed element of a personal injury claim. Often this is because an individual's care needs (and therefore costs) increase as they get older and their condition deteriorates. Even if an agreed position is reached, it must be accepted that there will always be a large range of outcomes around a given point estimate of longevity. It is an average and individuals will inevitably live longer or shorter than this. It therefore is an issue that falls to be addressed when it presents itself. The practical implications of any concessions made to an individual long after the claim has settled do however require to be considered and steps taken to ensure the best result is secured for the injured party.

In situations where concessions have been made in respect of life expectancy, which in turn impacts on the level of damages, but the injured party then ultimately exceeds their expected life expectancy, it follows that the award will be insufficient to last the injured party's lifetime. If a lump sum award is made in these circumstances, the likelihood is that it will simply run out and the fall back for care for example, will be onto local authority funded care, which may not meet all of their needs. This is not the ideal aim of a compensation claim. Similarly, in cases where an individual has a short life expectancy, the manner in which lump sum awards are expected to be invested over the injured party's lifetime and assumptions that are made are such that funds may not have long enough to perform and so never achieve the yield expected from investment, resulting in under compensation.

Equally, in cases where contributory negligence applies and in turn a percentage deduction has been applied to a lump sum award, there will never be enough compensation to last an injured party's lifetime even where life expectancy is not reduced.

In those scenarios, either (i) choices require to be made by the injured party (or their representatives) regarding how their compensation is spent to best suit their needs or (ii) riskier investment strategies require to be taken to try to inflate the investment return on their compensation to make it last as long as possible. Neither of these options are particularly palatable. It should be highlighted however that not all injured parties will be in the position to adopt an investment approach such as this or may be risk averse generally.

Ultimately, the issue being highlighted here is that not all cases fit into the neat scenario where a full award is made, no significant concessions have been made on life expectancy and sound investment decisions are taken over an individual's lifetime. A number of factors therefore need to be taken into account, which are unique to the injured party's case, when assessing compensation offers, particularly for future loss heads of claim. The key take away is that a lump sum award has the inevitable downside of the injured party having to assume the investment risk no matter the individual circumstances of the case.

The use of periodical payment orders can therefore be a useful tool to consider in cases with substantial future pecuniary losses. The pros and cons of periodical payment orders will be discussed more fully but particularly when the new rules of court come into force, greater options will be available for clients and for the courts to allow more flexibility and allow, in certain circumstances, for a fairer and fuller award to be made in these situations.

CHAPTER FOUR

PROBLEMS WITH FUTURE LOSS CALCULATIONS

Broadly, there are 2 main risks for a pursuer that must be considered when looking at lump sum awards: investment risk and longevity risk. When considering the merits of a lump award and a periodical payment order, it would be prudent to seek input from an actuary with experience in dealing with periodical payment orders and personal injury claims generally. An actuary can look at both of these risk factors from an actuarial perspective and provide a report, which can then be used by the independent financial advisor. The report from the independent financial advisor will still be required but this additional report will allow for more informed advice to be given on the merits of a periodical payment order or a traditional lump sum award.

The actuary will be able to prepare an impaired life table which shows the impact of the variability of life span around the expected life expectancy of the injured party. Essentially, it provides calculations on the chances of meeting or exceeding the expected life expectancy, which feeds into advice on quantum of the case. A more informed view can then be taken on what risks are acceptable to the injured party.

If this report was to be instructed, the actuary would need to be advised of the heads of claim which were to feature in the future annual payments to carry out these calculations. They would also have to have access to evidence relating to life expectancy of the injured party. This can be done at an early stage in the case when various

is evidence to demonstrate that it is not. Paragraph 8 of the Explanatory Notes of the Ogden Tables, 8th Edition, also states, "*...no further increase or reduction is required for mortality alone, unless there is clear evidence in an individual case that the individual is "atypical" and can be expected to experience a significantly shorter or longer than average lifespan, to an extent greater than would be encompassed by reasonable variations resulting from place of residence, lifestyle, education level, occupation and general health status*"

There is a body of case law emerging as to which medical experts are best placed to provide these views and whether statisticians still have a place in providing these opinions over clinicians but this is out with the scope of this book. When the injured party and their family members are faced with this evidence, it is often very difficult for them to accept. However, as practitioners for both pursuers and defenders, compromises often have to be made when cases are negotiated as it will become a decision for the court if an agreed position cannot be achieved. Divergence in opinion on life expectancy can often be the barrier in settling cases due to the major impact that it can have on the value of the case. Each case turns on its merits but particularly in cases where there are substantial annual care, therapy, case management, equipment and trust costs for example, the gulf in value between parties can be substantial. If a case is to settle in those circumstance, significant concessions would likely have to be made by both sides and that can be a difficult pill to swallow for both the injured party and insurers alike.

When life expectancy is disputed, periodical payment orders have their advantages: (i) periodical payments are made annually (unless otherwise agreed between parties), usually in December until the death of the injured party; (ii) the risk of compensation being exhausted due to issues over life expectancy is removed; (iii) the mechanism by which the payments are made also gives some comfort to insurers that individuals are not being over compensated if they die prior to their expected life expectancy; and (iv) this also gives comfort to the injured party and their families that if they exceed their life expectancy, the annual payment which is greatly needed for care and therapy for example, will continue if their needs increase as they age, until they die.

4.3 Risk/advantage of investing a lump sum early

By its nature and the manner in which lump sum payments are calculated, at least a large proportion of the award needs to be invested early to allow time for there to be a return. This feeds into the 100% compensation principle. Again, to reiterate the point, if the standard lump sum approach is taken, then the injured party assumes all of the investment risk.

They may however not be in the position to invest a large proportion of the award due to the need for significant capital expenditure upon settlement of the case being required. An example of this would be the purchase of accommodation.

Ultimately, a pursuer who is claiming in a personal injury claim is an atypical investor (see *Wells v Wells [1999] 1 AC 345*).

The broad spectrum of clients that pursue claims also has to be considered. Clients come from all walks of life, may be young or older which impacts on their needs and may or may not have experience of investing money. Those pursuing personal injury claims are often one-time litigants with little experience of dealing with large sums of money.

The injured party may also be incapable or require assistance with complex decision making resulting in the use of a guardian, trustee or power of attorney. In any situation where an injured party lacks capacity, they are vulnerable to exploitation whether that be inadvertent or deliberate. Steps can be taken to mitigate this but unfortunately, the risk is always there.

An added difficulty of lump sum awards is that if an injured party dies before the award is exhausted or a significant estate is left upon an individual's death, it is not the injured party who is benefiting from the compensation award. Instead, it would be their family members, who often can be the ones also making decisions as to how an award is being spent during the injured party's lifetime. That also can be an added risk factor on which decisions are being made and how compensation is being spent.

General poor decision making in relation to funds and their investment by either the individual themselves or their representatives, either deliberately or not also is a factor to consider. It is not uncommon for an individual with a traumatic brain injury to make poor financial decisions but this does not necessarily mean that they lack capacity. A protective measure in that scenario would be to establish a trust with either additional trusted family members as trustees or a professional trustee to protect the individual from any poor decisions that they may make on impulse. Those clients who have been seriously injured are often very vulnerable too, which means that agents must try to put in place protective measures as best they can in order to act in the client's best interests. Once a poor financial decision has been made, it is often difficult to undo, particularly if large sums of money are involved. This again can jeopardise the value of the lump sum award over time and the longevity of the award.

Even if poor decision making is not a factor, sometimes, even when reasonably sound decisions are made, funds simply do not perform as expected due to outside influences. This risk applies to any investment but poor performance of compensation funds will impact an injured party particularly severely, as they often do not have the option to recoup any losses through their employment or by other means.

4.4 Avoidance of investment risk

It used to be the case that the assumption was made that funds would be invested on a no-risk basis (*Wells v Wells [1999] 1 AC 345).* Now, the assumption is that the award will be invested in low-risk investments. The notional portfolio of investments should reflect the return that could reasonably expected to be achieved over 30 years after allowing for inflation (RPI) by an investor of no other financial resources, who is properly advised and who will make withdrawals to meet their losses and expenses. This causes issues for individuals who do not survive for the 30-year period after their accident.

This still leaves injured parties with the difficulty that they are still assuming some investment risk. The other financial element to this is that the injured party has to bear the cost of obtaining financial advice including the administrative costs and professional fees. That in itself can be expensive, particularly if it is required on an annual basis. Individuals will need sound investment advice and their views need to be taken into account. Different people will take different risks depending on their individual needs, their age and their requirements for the funds. By their nature, some risks taken will pay off and some will not. This may well suit certain individuals and they may want access to the lump sum after what can be a long claim process. It is a matter for individuals to do what they wish with their award but this does not always result in the award lasting in the way it should over their lifetime. The client may however strongly favour this approach and this is their reasoning for a lump sum award to be secured rather than a periodical payment order.

The use of a periodical payment order takes away this risk as the annual payments are guaranteed until the pursuer's death (subject to the terms of the agreement and the nature of the particular element of the annual payment). The annual payments are there to be spent on the care or case management needs that they incorporate. There is therefore no need to invest them. The lump sum which is agreed for other heads of claim, including past losses, is also smaller (than a standard entire lump sum award). This translates into what can be a more manageable size of initial award and risks taken with that award are diluted (in comparison to what they would be with an entire lump sum award) particularly if the investment return is not what was expected. There is however a practical drawback to this. Although *Swift v Carpenter* 2020 EWCA Civ 1295 has improved the situation for pursuers, it may still be that some other heads of claim require to be used to finance the accommodation element of the claim due to the lump sum being smaller in cases settled by means of a periodical payment order. This can be problematic for some pursuers and this is a practical implication of settling in this manner that must be considered.

CHAPTER FIVE

D'S PARENT & GUARDIAN (AP) V GREATER GLASGOW HEALTH BOARD [2011] CSOH 99

D's Guardian is a decision from the Outer House of the Court of Session, which was handed down on 16 June 2011. This case was of note because it highlighted the novel approach to settlement of this catastrophic injury case in Scotland. *D's Guardian* involved a young boy who sustained catastrophic neurological injuries at birth following a forceps delivery. His spinal cord was damaged at C1/C2, resulting in paralysis from the neck down. He required assistance with breathing and 24-hour care. It was anticipated that this would cost hundreds of thousands of pounds each year until his death. A key issue which had to be addressed by parties was difference in opinion of life expectancy experts, which had a significant impact on the value of the case depending on which approach was preferred. This was identified in the decision as a key difficulty in serious injury cases as this difference in forecasting life expectancy can result in a difference of millions of pounds in the valuation of the case over the pursuer's lifetime.

One must remember that the backdrop to this case was that periodic payment orders were introduced in England and Wales by the Courts Act 2003 but were not available as an option for the court to impose unilaterally in Scotland. A body of authority and practical experience was therefore being built up in England and Wales and this was, and still is, being looked on with interest by practitioners in Scotland.

D's Guardian was the first reported decision that set the scene for the introduction of periodical payment orders in Scotland. It was understood by the court that only one other medical negligence case in 2002 was settled by means of structured settlement. Section 2 of the Damages Act 1996 did however allow the court to make an order relating to a structured settlements provided that all parties agreed to it. They simply were not common at that time and this remains the case. As the Damages Act 1996 is the only legislation in force at present, this in itself is a stumbling block to the implementation of periodical payment orders if an agreement cannot be reached between parties (until part 2 of the Act and associated rules of court come into force). The court did however take this opportunity to comment on the use of periodical payment orders in Scotland and their practical application.

This case is a very useful starting point of reference for practitioners who are either considering or establishing a periodical payment order in their cases. A style periodical payment order agreement and style joint minute were appended to the judgement as a point of reference for other practitioners and these styles have continued to be used in practice. A word of caution: ensure that the styles are amended properly with the instruction of an experienced expert advisors if you are going to use them in your cases.

A point of note in *D's Guardian* is that there was a ratchet clause in the periodical payment agreement itself which prevented annual payments from being reduced in the event that the injured party's circumstances changed. This type of clause will however be a matter for negotiation. This is however a particularly useful clause from a pursuer's perspective as it provides more certainty to the annual payment. However, the Act allows for clauses to be included that will allow variation or suspension of the annual payment if certain conditions are met. Those provisions must however be written into the periodical payment agreement. This highlights the potential battleground that agents face when agreeing the specific terms of the periodical payment order agreement itself as clauses of this nature could have a massive financial impact if the situation changes for the pursuer.

Lord Stewart did issue some words of caution to practitioners at paragraph 28 in *D's Guardian* even at that stage:

> *"At least in cases where self-funding packages are available, lawyers who fail to address the merits of compensation by periodical payments could now be liable in professional negligence for resulting losses."*

Lord Stewart provides some interesting commentary on the use of periodical payment awards and comments on the need for different indexing depending on the circumstances of the award. He also offers the view that lump sum awards may still be the preferred settlement model of choice if there is settlement at a discounted sum, whether that be due to liability issues or because of the application of contributory negligence (see paragraph 29).

In practice, this is not quite so straightforward, particularly if life expectancy is compromised. Even in a situation where there will be a deduction for either contributory negligence or a discounted settlement, the best approach may still be to settle by means of a periodical payment order once financial advice is taken. This is however dependent on a number of factors that will be discussed more fully later.

As a nod to what was to come, this decision also highlighted the need for amendment (applicable in Scotland) to section 2 of the Damages Act 1996 to allow courts the power to impose periodical payment orders in appropriate cases. The Scottish Government had an amendment to the Damages Act 1996 under consideration at the time of this decision and this legislation had now been drafted in the form of the Act.

CHAPTER SIX

THE OPERATION OF PERIODICAL PAYMENT ORDERS

A periodical payment order is in essence a structured settlement, which is governed by the terms of the periodical payment order agreement executed by both parties. It is comprised of what would be a smaller lump sum payment initially upon settlement and then annual payments thereafter, usually in December of each year, until death of the injured party (or an otherwise agreed date, which also could include bi-annual or quarterly payments). The reason that they usually are paid in December is due to the annual date of publication of the various indices used for calculation of the updated annual payments each year. This is usually in November of each year and therefore time is allowed to recalculate payments before the annual payment is made.

Depending on when the periodical payment order is agreed and payment made, parties will also require to consider whether a pro-rata payment up to when the first annual payment is to be made is appropriate. This would require to be clearly set out in the agreement.

At present, parties agree which heads of claim will go into the periodical payment order. This need not be all future pecuniary losses. The Act, once in force, will also allow for future losses in whole or in part to be put into the periodical payment order agreement. This will be case dependent but adds a further layer of flexibility to this mode of settlement. The idea is that periodical payments orders are needs based and the pursuer should not be left in the situation where they cannot afford to pay for their needs over their lifetime even if they change (provided that it is granted on a full liability basis). Depending on the heads of claim being included in the annual payment, some elements of the annual payment will last longer than others for example, care costs will continue for life but not all future pecuniary losses do and may stop at a certain date. This will all require to be carved out in the agreement.

It is a requirement that the agreement (or court award in the future) must set out the specific level of annual payment and that the payment is broken down in the agreement itself. For example, the agreement should specifically state the separate annual sums being awarded for (i) rehabilitation costs, (ii) care costs, (iii) case management costs and (iv) trusts costs if those were the future losses being included in the order. It is likely rare for future loss of earnings to be included in the annual payments. The agreement will also require to state the duration of these payments, when they will be paid if it is more than once per annum and the index to which the payment is being linked. If there is agreement that payments will increase or decrease at a certain time, then this should also be specified in the agreement in detail i.e. the date when these payments will change and the amount that they will be changed to. The key is for the agreement to be specific insofar as the terms of the agreement are clear to all parties.

At present, the practice is to append the executed agreement to the final interlocutor of court interposing authority to a joint minute. As discussed, styles for both the agreement and the joint minute itself can be found in *D's Guardian.*

It is important that steps are taken to allow enforcement in the future if necessary if there is default. It is therefore prudent to register the agreement in the Books of Council and Session and until rules of court are in force further governing the use of periodical payment orders, it should always be appended to the final interlocutor.

As touched upon previously, future pecuniary losses such as care and equipment costs and trust costs would be the sorts of heads of claim subject to the future annual payments. Until the rules of court come into force and a case actually proceeds to a hearing, it is a matter for the parties to decide which heads of claim (even for future pecuniary losses) are captured by the periodical payment order.

A real positive for using periodical payment orders is that the agreement can be structured in a way which allows for flexibility in the event that an individual's needs change in the future. These terms can all be written into the agreement itself.

It should be noted however that the multiplier/multiplicand approach for calculating future losses does not change when settling by means of a periodical payment order. The issues of retirement age; future capacity for earnings, an individual's career trajectory and the time when care needs may require to step up still require to be either negotiated or decided upon by court in the usual way. These are always difficult decisions and the same expert evidence is required when preparing cases such as this as if you were going to take the traditional lump sum approach.

6.1 Removing uncertainty regarding life expectancy;

As previously discussed, the issue of life expectancy is particularly problematic when valuing serious injury claims if there is divergence of expert opinion. The nature of a periodical payment order is such that this factor is taken out of the equation. This is particularly useful when acting for an individual who was relatively young at the time of the accident as the annual payments are guaranteed until death. As part of the agreement, proof of life, such as a certificate from the injured party's GP after examination would have to be disclosed to the insurer/paying party each year prior to the annual payment being made (see the English case of *Wallace v Follett [2013] EWCA Civ 146* for discussion of this point).

This certainty of payment can also provide some comfort to their family members as a young injured party's care needs will likely continue after their parents' deaths. The increase in care costs in the event of parents' death/ill health if they were carers is usually dealt with by means of a step-up clause in the agreement itself. Accordingly, they will have the security of ongoing annual payments to fund their care needs even if they live past their life expectancy. Given the advancements in medical care, there is always a distinct possibility that this may happen.

Removing the issue of life expectancy also gives comfort to the insurers in light of the inherent difficulty of predicting when someone will die. Invariably, any expert evidence on this point will likely be wrong. It takes away the concern of over-compensation or the family being left significant sums as inheritance if the injured party dies sooner than expected.

6.2 Guaranteed secure tax-free index linked payments for life;

Payments made under a periodical payment order are tax free. Separate input should be obtained from a solicitor specialising in trusts on tax implications if the injured party is not the sole beneficiary. It should be remembered that income generated from interest payments from invested sums will however be taxable, even if the initial traditional lump sum award is not. The annual payments are also index linked to the appropriate index depending on what professional service is being provided to the injured party i.e. ASHE 6115 for care workers. This will usually result in increased payments being made over time. This is important to ensure that real money terms are being reflected in future payments made. Submissions will require to be made as to the most appropriate index to be used for whichever element of the annual payment it applies to and it ultimately will be a matter for the court. It is crucial that practitioners take advice from experienced independent financial advisers over which index would be most suitable for the type of annual payment being included in the periodical payment order. ASHE and RPI are the main indices used that have successfully been applied in England and Wales.

The English Court of Appeal decision of *Tameside & Glossip Acute Services NHS Trust v Thompstone [2008] EWCA Civ 5* was a landmark decision in respect of the use of indexing for annual payments. It held that difference indices could be used for future losses. The type of index used is at the discretion of the court. Prior to this, there were a number of decisions which dealt with the question of the appropriateness of the RPI index for annual payment calculations. This case changed the law from the general use of RPI indexing for care payments to linking them to ASHE, which has allowed for a fairer and more realistic approach to future professional services payments. Prior to this decision, in England, RPI linked payments for all services were the norm, which would have likely resulted in underpayment of care costs in the future as different profession's salaries increased over time. Had RPI payments continued to be used then this likely would have meant that future payments would not have been reflective of the real money costs of care over time. RPI looks at the change in price of goods and services for a household rather than looking at actual salaries of employees from a number of different sectors (which is how ASHE is computed). It may also have led to the reduction in the use of periodical payment orders instead of lump sum awards due to the risk of under-compensation.

The difficulty with relying on RPI is that wage rates often increase faster than prices. The choice of index is therefore an important one. ASHE has the benefit of having a number of sub categories for different types of workers within it and it also reports on both annual and hourly rates of pay. It remains to be seen which indices will be employed by the judiciary but at present, it is a matter for agreement between parties. Caution should be taken in employing too many different indices as this may complicate matters further. The key point is to ensure that the appropriate index is used and not to take a broad-brush approach to this. Instead, real thought should be applied to the outcome you want to achieve from the annual payments.

6.3 Avoidance of risk

In the vast majority of cases, the injured party is a one-time litigant. The importance of taking the client's wishes into account in this regard is very important. As every individual is unique, they will have their own views regarding risk and what risks they are willing to take both in the context of litigation and investment of their compensation payment. The potential change in the discount rate is also a factor to consider here, particularly if a case is approaching settlement when the new discount rate is expected. It should be remembered however that the court could take this decision out of parties' hands if it thinks that a periodical payment order will best serve the interests of all parties. That is not however the case at present.

A real benefit of periodical payment orders is that the risk element of how settlement funds will perform over the injured party's lifetime is significantly reduced for them. The insurer ultimately is being passed back this risk. The risk element of both investment of the initial lump sum is also reduced because it is smaller than what it would be if a lump sum payment was made. The certainty of future payments at a value which is in real money terms is also an attractive feature of periodical payment orders.

The security of payment will be discussed later but this is also an important feature of the legislation that will govern these orders. Agents must satisfy themselves that the future of annual payments are 'reasonably secure'. There is a body of case law in England and Wales which has developed over time, which gives guidance on the reasonable security of payments but in essence, if there is doubt over whether the funding party will be able to make these payments in say 50 or 60 years' time, then a periodical payment order should not be agreed to or made.

The very nature of a periodical payment order results in the injured party being tied to the insurer for their lifetime. Again, it depends on the injured party's attitude to this. This may not be attractive to them or they may see it as a risk that something may happen resulting in payments not being made in the future. This risk is potentially heightened when there are a number if insurers party to the periodical payment agreement, if there are multiple defenders in the action. Insurers will require to ensure that there will be sufficient cash flow available in the future to guarantee these payments. They may also have to have some sort of agreement in the background if, in this scenario, one insurer is unable to make payment in the future. In the event that the compensator is regulated by the Financial Services Compensation Scheme, failure to make payment would be covered by this. Reassurance requires to be given to the client so that they understand how insurers will fund these payments, so that they have comfort that they will not be left in the situation where they will only receive partial payment of compensation over their lifetime. This will be of particular significance when the court has the unilateral power to grant these orders.

6.4 Interim payments

Interim payments are a key feature of serious injury cases. The level of interim payment sought is however always a balancing act depending on the heads of claim and value of the case overall. Unless rehabilitation is agreed on a joint basis under the Rehabilitation Code 2015, this is one of the main reasons for an early interim payment being sought by agents for the injured party. It may also be that a more general interim payment is required for living costs when the injured party is unable to work, where there is an accommodation claim or a care regime that requires to be trialled before parties agree to its implementation. Serious injury cases also often take a significant amount of time to resolve depending on their circumstances and it is not unreasonable to require interim damages.

As is the case where any interim payment is sought, the level of the interim payment is restricted by the potential for a finding of a high percentage of contributory negligence. This remains a consideration when seeking an interim payment when a periodical payment order is being considered.

Securing interim payments does not preclude settlement by means of a periodical payment order and should not be seen as a barrier to it. However, the size of interim payment secured should not be so large that it impacts on the ability to settle (or the ability of the court to make an award) by means of a periodical payment order. It is often the case that parties do not know whether settlement in this manner is attractive until the injured party has seen more of a recovery and expert reports have been obtained. Even if accommodation is purchased for example, this is an asset that may provide a source of income in the future. It is also generally accepted that the accommodation claim will form part of the lump sum award. An example of how the court may approach the calculation of an interim payment against the backdrop of a periodical payment order can be found in *Cobham Hire Services Limited v Benjamin Eles (By his Mother and Litigation Friend) [2009] EWCA 204*. A conservative approach to the valuation of the case is adopted when interim payments are being awarded by court but an important feature is that a reasonable view has to be taken as to which heads would comprise the initial lump sum payment and the heads that would likely be put into the periodical payment order annual payments. A decision can then be taken regarding what is reasonable as an interim payment when comparing this to the initial lump sum award that a court may make in the context of the periodical payment order. The recent case of *AL v A [2021] EWHC 1761 (QB)* is a further example of the court's approach to interim payments, even when their value was significant. The whole context of the claim and overall value are important considerations.

In the situation where liability is disputed, it may be that any settlement discussions are not taking place until close to the date of the diet of proof. A decision may still not have been made regarding preference for settlement by means of a lump sum award or periodical payment order. It may be that the pursuer wants to keep their options open depending on how the settlement negotiations proceed.

The practical steps that require to be taken here are simply for interim payments to be recorded in the periodical payment order itself and for these sums to be included as a consideration when the initial lump sum is being agreed/awarded by court once the court can do this. As is the case with any interim payment, it will eat into the final settlement payment. The implication of this is perhaps felt more harshly by the injured party when a periodical payment order is used as the initial lump sum payment is always smaller than it would have been had a traditional lump sum award been negotiated.

CHAPTER SEVEN

PERIODICAL PAYMENT ORDERS IN PRACTICE UNDER THE DAMAGES (INVESTMENT RETURNS AND PERIODICAL PAYMENTS) (SCOTLAND) ACT

Once the rules of court have been published and part 2 of the Act is in force, the court will have the flexibility to impose periodical payment orders even against parties' wishes. However, the court should still have special regard to the pursuer's needs and preferences when doing so under section 3 of the Act. It is hoped that this would only happen in rare situations, but this remains unknown. It is likely that authorities in England and Wales will be considered when determining the appropriateness of a periodical payment order but Scottish courts will require to pave their own way in applying this legislation. A body of Scottish case law will develop over time and this will require to be done responsibly to ensure that flexibility remains when settling/making awards in serious injury cases. It is paramount that the individual circumstances of each case remain at the heart of decision making, resulting in the best form of order to meet the injured party's needs. The binding nature of decisions from certain courts and the ability to set precedent means that the judiciary must use this power wisely once the Act is fully in force.

It is hoped that if an injured party has (i) had appropriate financial advice regarding a lump sum award versus a periodical payment order, (ii) has capacity and (iii) is not behaving in a way that is manifestly unreasonable, but prefers one form of award over another and (iv) provides reasons for this, that the court will follow the pursuer's preference. That however remains to be seen and there likely will be situations where a periodical payment order is imposed notwithstanding the pursuer's preferences if the court considers that it is in the pursuer's best interests and that it would best meet their needs.

7.1 Obligation to consider periodical payments

The Act amends section 2 of the Damages Act 1996:

- Section 3(1) of the Act obliges the court to consider periodical payment orders when awarding damages for future pecuniary losses only – it cannot make an order relating to past losses unless all parties consent;

- The periodical payment order can deal with future pecuniary losses in whole or in part;

- The court must have special regard to the injured party's needs and preferences when doing so;

- The court may make an order of this nature with or without the consent of the parties to the action.

- It is anticipated that the rules of court or a practice note will be issued which sets out the factors to be taken into account. In England, the court's considerations include (i) how much the annual payment will be, (ii) the reasoning the injured party has for their preferences including what financial advice has been secured by them and (iii) the reasoning the defender has for their preference. It is hoped that the preference of the pursuer will carry more weight that the preference of the defender as ultimately it is their compensation at the end of the day.

- The Court will also consider contributory negligence when deciding upon whether a periodical payment order is the best way to dispose of the case and how this impacts on the level of damages an injured party will receive.

7.2 Continuity of Payment

Section 3(1)(c) of the Act goes on to provide that a periodical payment order can only be granted if the court is satisfied the continuity of payment under the order is 'reasonably secure.' This simply means that the compensator will be able to make payment annually for the duration of the order, which could be many years into the future.

The security of the defender will be considered in the value for money report prepared by the independent financial advisor. Agents must be mindful that it is not only insurers that may be the compensator. It could be health boards or government bodies. There is a raft of English authority dealing with the security of various defenders. An example of this is *YM v Gloucestershire Hospital NHS Foundation Trust [2006] EWHC 820 (QB)* which held an NHS trust to be reasonably secure.

An interesting situation arises post Brexit when the Motor Insurers Bureau is considered as it is not a member of the Financial Services Compensation Scheme. The English decisions of *Thacker v Steeples, 6 May 2005, Cox J, unreported* and *Bennett v Stephens [2010] EWHC 2194 (QB)* did however hold the MIB to be reasonably secure due to its longevity and its substantial resources in light of the membership of a large number of insurers. It also relied upon Article 4 of the European Directive on motor insurance as the MIB is the body through which victims of uninsured and untraced drivers are compensated. Even post Brexit, it is considered that it is unlikely that the government or insurers members would allow the MIB to fail to meet its obligations due to its history and the reason for its establishment. However, this cannot be guaranteed and it is wise to seek further assurances from the MIB if a periodical payment order is being considered.

There is further detail in the Act relating to the bodies that would be automatically determined as reasonably secure, which includes (i) part of the Scottish administration, and (ii) Crown and government bodies. It also includes a scheme under section 213 of the Financial Services and Markets Act 2000. This therefore removes the need for the paying body to prove that they are reasonably secure. The Act also allows for the Scottish government to add in, through regulations a particular category of health service body or non-government body, so it remains to be seen which bodies may be included in this manner.

Under the Act, the court will be able to order the compensator to make payment in a specified way or if it is not persuaded that continuity of payment is reasonably secure, order the compensator to take specific steps to secure the continuity of payment. Steps could include ordering the paying body to purchase an annuity to cover the obligations within a periodical payment order. However, these options are likely to be limited and insurers likely will have to self-fund periodical payment orders for practical reasons.

7.3 Index linking of payments

Section 3 of the Act also deals with index linking of periodical payments. It is deemed to be included in the order that payments will alter and when they will but further specification on this will come from the rules of court. The Act does provide for different indices being used depending on the nature of payments being made as is the case in England. As was the case in *D's Guardian*, it would however be prudent to negotiate a clause which ensures that the payments will never reduce from the initial agreed annual payment even if the index falls over time.

7.4 Variation or suspension of future pecuniary loss award

Section 4 of the Act makes provision for the ability for an application to be made to the court by one or all parties for variation or suspension of payments if certain circumstances are met. It also provides for the lifting of suspended payments where certain circumstances are met. The principle underpinning these provisions is to ensure that the injured party is not under or over compensated. This is not a general power to vary the order when something unforeseen happens. It is anticipated that very specific criteria will require to be met before the court would vary the order. However, if parties intend to rely upon variation to the agreement, then there must be a specific provision that allows for it in the agreement otherwise, the agreement cannot be revised in the future.

The court will only be able to exercise this power to include provision to vary or suspend the award if (i) the injured party may experience a change in physical or mental condition at some point in the future (whether the timeframe is known or not) and (ii) if the change does occur, it will result in significant under or over-compensation from the annual payment for future pecuniary losses. It is likely that the court will not grant a variation to the periodical payment order if it is only a small change to the pursuer's condition that does not have significant financial impact. Similarly, at the stage of making a periodical payment order, it is unlikely that the court would allow provision for variation if it is just a fanciful risk or chance of a change in condition occurring. Certainty of award still is an important factor for the pursuer and their families so the use of variation or suspension provisions will require to be considered carefully and caution taken if this clause was to be included in the agreement.

The court will require to specify the type of physical or mental change that is to occur before an application to vary or suspend payment can be made. Provision can also be made as to the period of time the parties have to make this application. The court will only have the power to do this when there is provision in the agreement/court award to do this. It is not a power that can be exercised freely. There is greater detail in the Act which looks at the finer points of variation and suspension of orders.

There is potential for this sort of provision to be hotly contested between parties. The power to vary the periodical payment has an inherent flexibility which, depending on the circumstances, might be attractive to parties but the certainty of future payments is reduced.

It is anticipated that situations such as (i) the development of epilepsy (see *Farrugia v Burkenshaw & Ors 2014 EWHC 1036 (QB)* as an English example of a case where variation of the order was discussed in the context of the risk of epilepsy and the security of payment was also decided upon), (ii) change in educational needs or (iii) a change from gratuitous care to paid care would merit a variation to the award. Similarly, an injured party may deteriorate as they age resulting in increased care costs. A change in medical condition resulting in an increase in medical, rehabilitation or care costs or a requirement for increased capital expenditure would also be when a variation provision would be of use. A provision like this could be really useful particularly when there would be a significant increase in care costs for example. It does however mean that there is scope for both parties to make this application in the future. That may or may not be desirable depending on the facts of the case.

From a practical perspective, it is important that both the agents' and insurer's files are retained until at least the period for variation has expired and if there is no agreed period for that, indefinitely until the injured party's death. Papers from the original case will become pertinent to any variation order, which may happen decades into the future and therefore require to be retained.

It should be remembered that the step up in costs may also be able to be built into the periodical payment order itself without the need for provision for a variation order. An example of that might be where medical evidence anticipates that there will be a step up in care needs when the individual reaches a certain age. If the traditional lump sum award approach is used, that could result in harder fought negotiations if there is a dispute in expert evidence or over life expectancy. The benefit of a periodical payment order is that annual payments are guaranteed until death. If the conflicting evidence is correct from the defenders, then the pursuer will not reach the age where the step up in care is triggered and it will not be an issue. If the pursuer does however, then the pursuer has guaranteed secure payments and the security of full payment for these costs. The latter scenario should carry more weight when the 100% compensation principle is considered.

7.5 Expenses

When this legislation was drafted, there was concern over whether the pursuer would have to pay for the expenses associated with variation of the periodical payment order. Section 5 of the Act deals with expenses in respect of qualifying or appeal proceedings for the periodical payment order. No expenses will be awarded against the injured party unless the injured party conducts these proceedings in an inappropriate manner. This will be determined against the backdrop of the section 8 of the Litigation (Expenses and Group Proceedings) (Scotland) Act 2018. The terms of this legislation would allow for expenses to be awarded against the pursuer where either the pursuer or their representative makes a fraudulent representation or acts fraudulently in connection with proceedings; behaves in a way that is manifestly unreasonable or behaves in a manner that the court considers is an abuse of process. The standard of proof is that of balance of probabilities. Qualifying proceedings would relate to variation or suspension of the order. Appeal proceedings would arise from any of the qualifying proceedings. Expenses generally when dealing with periodical payment orders will be discussed later.

7.6 Assignation and Insolvency

Section 6 of the Act deals with the restriction on assignation of rights to receive periodical payments. An assignation will have no effect unless it is approved by the court. The court will only approve the assignation in special circumstances. This sub section does not apply to periodical payment orders granted before these provisions come into force. Further detail regarding these provisions can be found in the Act.

Section 7 deals with insolvency and should be considered in full in the event that this situation arises. The detail is contained within the Act and is complex but generally, the use of periodical payments is looked on more favourably than general assets in an insolvency situation.

PART II

CONSIDERATIONS

CHAPTER EIGHT

LUMP SUM V PERIODICAL PAYMENT ORDERS

The aim of this book is not to suggest that one mode of settlement is better than the other on a blanket basis. Given the terms of the legislation and once it is in force, the takeaway is that the potential for disposal of the case by means of a periodical payment order cannot be ignored. It must be dealt with in the context of advice being given by agents acting for both pursuers and defenders. Even now, this should still be a pertinent consideration as they can be agreed extra-judicially. In England and Wales, the benchmark for periodical payment orders seems to be around £1 million but it is apparent that depending on the case, cases with a value of over £500,000 may still be suitable for periodical payment orders. From both a practical and risk management point of view, agents should have a clear record of advice given regarding periodical payments and the client's reaction to them. It should never be in doubt that advice has been given in respect of the prospect of periodical payment orders particularly when the rules of court come into force.

As touched upon previously, the attitude of the injured party is a key consideration but it is not the only one. An obvious consideration where a periodical payment order may not be appropriate is where compensation is not being paid on a full liability basis due to the application of contributory negligence or when an economic offer is being made to resolve matters, even if it is sizeable. Unless an individual has other funds available to make up the shortfall, then funds will never cover all losses. It also could be that local authority funding of care still continues even when some care is being bought in but that will depend on the local authority where the injured party lives, even if a trust is established. This is another factor that needs to be considered when choosing the most appropriate model of settlement.

In these situations, a lump sum award may well be the best option for the injured party as this will give them a larger sum to invest upon settlement of the claim and hopefully, if riskier investments are taken or difficult choices made about how the compensation is spent, then funds may last longer and perform better over their lifetime even compared to a periodical payment order. That is never the ideal situation for an injured party to be in but often it is the reality of the situation.

It is not always the case however that even when there is a deduction for contributory negligence, that a party should not consider a periodical payment order. Contributory negligence could be a reasonably small deduction and if life expectancy is disputed, then it may still be the better option to secure longevity of damages until the injured party's death. This would be a particularly attractive option when the injured party is young as it would allow certainty of payment over their lifetime.

8.1 Advantages of a periodical payment order

- Less risk for the pursuer e.g. mortality, investment and other practical risks when dealing with investment of a lump sum payment.

- Less risk is more attractive to a risk averse pursuer.

- Periodical payments are income tax free whereas income from an invested sum is taxable.

- Smaller amounts of money are easier to manage on a practical level than one large lump sum award for the pursuer. There may be less worry attached to managing these sums.

- If life expectancy is reduced, certainty of payment until death is guaranteed.

- A reduced life expectancy, which is a key factor in the negotiation of the lump sum award becomes less of an issue.

- If there is a change in the injured party's circumstances resulting in additional funds being required, whether that is the risk of development of a condition or contingent upon other factors, this can be built into the agreement.

- If there is a step up in care needs (and in turn associated costs), a periodical payment can provide for that if the injured party reaches the age that this will take place.

- The concern regarding over payment of compensation is diluted for the NHS (or other State financed body) or insurer as payments cease upon death.

- If variation or suspension is built into the agreement, this adds flexibility to both parties.

- The risk of abuse of funds either deliberately or inadvertently is reduced as the initial lump sum award is smaller and even if one annual payment is used irresponsibly, the injured party will be protected to an extent because a further payment will be made the next year.

- Future payments are index linked to the appropriate index ensuring that future payments will be enough to cover the costs negotiated or awarded for professional services.

- The NHS (or other State financed body) or insurer will not require to fund a large lump sum award upon settlement and that may well suit their needs form a commercial perspective.

8.2 Disadvantages of a periodical payment order

- The injured party is tied to the NHS (or other State financed body) or insurer for their lifetime.

- if the litigation has been very contentious, this may not be attractive to a pursuer or the pursuer may simply not want this tie to exist and would prefer to sever links on settlement.

- The injured party loses the choice of how to spend the entire lump sum payment and the flexibility that goes with that. Ultimately, it is up to the pursuer to spend their compensation in the manner in which they see fit once a case has concluded.

- If a reduced settlement payment is made due to liability issues, there will never be sufficient funds available over the injured party's lifetime to pay for all of their needs.

- The injured party will require to attend their GP to be examined and to obtain proof of life, which requires to be exhibited annually to the insurer prior to payment (See *Wallace v Follett* [2013] EWCA Civ 146 for discussion around the provision of proof of life certificates/medical examinations).

- The calculation of the index linked payment will be done each year after the appropriate index is published. The injured party will require to pay for and deal with the administration of this calculation being checked if they wish to do so. Although generally index linked payment will increase, they could also decrease over time in line with the index used to calculate the value of the payment (unless a clause is agreed to prevent that from happening).

- It is imperative that the most appropriate index is used for future annual payments. It may be that there is judicial discretion in this regard so agents will require to be aware of the different options available and be in the position to lead evidence from experts on this point in court.

- Agents must ensure that funds are reasonably secure and the potential for non-payment in the future may be a source of anxiety for the pursuer, even if the chance is small.

- There is more administration to be done by both parties if a periodical payment order is granted.

- Statutory funding of care may be jeopardised if a periodical payment order is used depending on where the pursuer lives and the relevant local authorities' approach – this all remains to be determined once periodical payment orders are used more regularly in Scotland.

- The initial lump sum payment is smaller than with a traditional lump sum award. This is important if interim payments and success fees also require to be deducted, which reduces the payment further. This must be balanced with the overall benefit of the use of the periodical payment order.

- If suspension or variation clauses are built into the periodical payment order, then this is something the injured party will always have to be mindful of throughout their life and this may not always be to their benefit. If provisions allow and the pursuer's condition improves, then a variation of the periodical payment order could be sought from the court by the defenders.

- For the NHS (or other State financed body) or insurer, the actual cost over time of the annual payments is not certain and there is no known end date for payments to cease. Their exposure is therefore an unknown entity.

- The NHS (or other State financed body) or insurer must ensure that they have sufficient funds to pay for annual payments into the future.

8.3 Summary

The advantages and disadvantages of each settlement model should be considered by agents before providing advice to clients on settlement of their case or proceeding to a full evidential hearing. As discussed, a report from an actuary dealing with investment risk and longevity of the award from an actuarial perspective can be useful alongside the report from the independent financial advisor.

From a practical perspective, and at present, if the defenders agree to it, it can be useful to have offers made as (i) a full lump sum award or (ii) as a periodical payment order (with the initial lump sum award and annual payments thereafter). In essence, 2 different types of offer are being made. It may be that the defenders are willing to increase payments into the annual payment for the periodical payment order, which is in turn more beneficial to the injured party, if a periodical payment order is agreed upon between parties during settlement negotiations. The reason for this is because it may be the compensator's preferred method of settlement. This defers payment over a longer period of time and that may well suit the compensator. Consideration requires to be given to the full lump sum award and the periodical payment order separately and their terms compared if the defender is prepared to make different offers on these different settlement models. Defenders cannot however be forced to make 2 different forms of offer to allow for comparison at present particularly as there is no mechanism to force a periodical payment order in court or to tender on that basis.

CHAPTER NINE

IFA – VALUE FOR MONEY REPORTS

When dealing with periodical payment orders and comparing them to traditional lump sum awards, agents should call upon those with financial expertise in this area before providing advice to the injured party. It is not imperative but it is prudent. The appropriate expert here is an IFA in conjunction with an experienced actuary to look at the risks from an actuarial perspective. The IFA could be retained for future investment advice, which would be more costly than their initial input into the negotiation phase of the case. As periodical payment orders are relatively uncommon in Scotland at present, but likely to become more prevalent, it is useful to instruct an IFA with Scottish offices but also with representation in England. The reason for this is that English IFAs are now well versed in dealing with the financial aspects of periodical payment orders and if they are experienced in this field, they will have a working knowledge of the relevant English authorities too. They will also have experience of the impact of different indices being used for different types of heads of claim, which will be very useful when either presenting evidence in court or during negotiations. Care should be taken when selecting the IFA to ensure that they have the appropriate expertise in this area.

9.1 The value for money report

The type of report to be instructed when a periodical payment order offer is made is a value for money report. The benefit of instructing an IFA is that they are FCA compliant. They have the skill set which allows advice to be taken on risk and return for the pursuer and they can check the calculations being implemented in the agreement and any relevant dates in the agreement. They cannot however look at calculations from an actuarial perspective which is why the additional actuarial report is required. They also could be approached to carry out a check on the annual payment calculations following publication of the new indices if the client wishes to instruct them to do that. In practice, if the annual payment changes due to changes in the indices used, then the pursuer will be advised of this in advance of the annual payment being made. This would be when a check of the calculation could be carried out.

It is anticipated that the court will require sight of evidence that the value of the periodical payment order and the reasonableness of its use has been considered fully by agents. A value for money report is the manner in which to do this. It also allows the injured party to fully consider their options. If a lump sum offer is made, its value can be projected into the future and information provided as to when funds will be exhausted. If required, the IFA can seek their own input from an actuary to assist with those calculations or practitioners could instruct it separately. Those figures are then compared to the value of the periodical payment order offer and the differences explained in the report. In essence, an expert view is being provided as to suitability of the periodical payment order against a traditional lump sum award. If a lump sum award is not made to allow this comparison to take place, IFAs can be instructed to provide their view as to what an equivalent lump sum award would be deduced from the periodical payment order offer's terms.

It is likely to be negligent if agents do not obtain this type of report and moreover will be expected by court in any event when periodical payment orders are being considered.

9.2 An IFA's role in settlement negotiations

From a practical standpoint, it can be very useful if the IFA is present at the pre-trial meeting or settlement meeting in the event that different offers are being made. The useful aspect of this is initial general advice is immediately available during negotiations. The IFA can also take this opportunity to set out the pros and cons of a periodical payment order from a financial perspective when considering that individual's needs. They will be able to discuss their attitude to risk and form a view of the best settlement model from a financial perspective. This allows the pursuer to have fully informed advice when any decisions are being taken. The report itself would be prepared after the event but their presence is useful during these meetings.

Even if they are not present and instead considering a periodical payment order offer which was made to agents directly, the IFA would need to speak to the injured party to form a view on the suitability of the periodical payment order for them. The reason for this is that these points are discussed in detail in their reports.

9.3 Summary

This is an important step when providing advice on a periodical payment order. It is important evidence when presenting the suitability and viability of the periodical payment order either to court or to your client. Explaining a periodical payment order to either a client with serious injuries or their representatives can be a difficult exercise as it is complicated but it is imperative that they are fully informed either before making a decision to settle their case or, once the rules come into force, walking into a court room. Finally, the IFA (and actuary if instructed) will require to be certified as an expert upon the conclusion of the case to ensure recovery of fees for their involvement in the case. It is likely that these reports will not be excessively expensive as they will have standardised reports that could be used from other cases and there are standardised agreements that can be used and amended. The costly element of this for the client would be any ongoing involvement that an IFA would have after the case has settled.

CHAPTER TEN

ANCILLARY CONSIDERATIONS: TRUSTS/CAPACITY/BENEFITS/LOCAL AUTHORITY STATUTORY PROVISION OF FUNDING FOR CARE

Serious injury cases often require input from specialists in their field and their involvement is an important factor to ensure that the injured party is securing the best advice available.

10.1 Trusts

It is encouraged that, when it is appropriate to do so, specialist advice is sought from a solicitor specialising in trust law regarding (i) whether a trust should be established, and (ii) the best form of trust to suit the needs of the individual. Steps should also be taken to best protect the means tested benefits and local authority funding of care through the establishment of a trust in appropriate cases. Particularly if interim payments are being sought, it is prudent to obtain this advice at an early stage in the case and to obtain funding from the defenders (if it is appropriate to do so if trusts costs will be a recoverable head of claim) to allow it to be established. Trusts costs can be included in the annual periodical payments and therefore independent evidence is required on the costs of both establishing the trust and its administration into the future. Usually, trust costs are higher in the initial years post settlement and once trustees settle into their role, they can reduce over time but still remain a significant head of claim. Trusts costs can escalate quickly depending on the complexity of the trust and professional trustees' involvement, so it is prudent to obtain an expert report on these costs from a different solicitor than the one who established the trust as a check and balance to future costs. The annual periodical payment can easily be paid into the trust too and this is written into the agreement itself. The trust would however require to be set up in advance of signing of the agreement and settlement funds being received.

10.2 Capacity

In Scotland, you will be aware that there are different methods of protecting clients who are vulnerable, have varying capacity or are incapable. These include but are not limited to powers of attorney being granted or guardianship order being sought. It is important to ensure that the person giving instructions in this situation is permitted to do so in line with the legal document or order appointing them and this should be checked by agents. This also applies to who signs the periodical payment order agreement. It is also crucial that where possible, the views of the injured party are taken into account, particularly if they differ from their representative and they retain a degree of capacity. Capacity is a specialist area and it should not be forgotten about. Specialist advice must be sought in appropriate cases.

10.3 Benefits

If an individual has been seriously injured as a result of an accident, they likely will be in receipt of benefits. Agents must be mindful of the impact of an award of compensation on means tested benefits and advice given to the client certainly to seek specialist advice upon receipt of damages. This advice should have been provided in any event when considering offsetable benefits against certain heads of claim and when interim payments. This advice can be provided by welfare rights advisors or sometimes private client or trusts lawyers. Clients should be signposted about the impact of compensation on their benefits in any event. It is likely that periodical payments will not impact upon means tested benefits but again, as this is new territory for Scotland, this remains to be seen and an added layer of protection through the establishment of a trust should be considered.

10.4 Local Authority Funded Care

The periodical payment order agreement will deal with any claw back provisions and the compensation's interaction with local authority funded care. All of this is subject to negotiation and this is an area that requires to be fully investigated to ensure that full compensation is secured where possible. It is important to contact the local authority to try to find out what their position will be on the provision of statutory funded care in the future in the event of a successful compensation claim (settled by means of a periodical payment order). Each local authority tends to have their own policy in this regard and likely the response will be that each case turns on its merits and the position may change in the future. Attempts to secure this information should be made in any event so that it can be considered by both the injured party and during settlement negotiations. The terms of the periodical payment order itself also should be carefully considered to ensure that it reflects what was negotiated between parties.

CHAPTER ELEVEN

EXPENSES

The Act makes provisions relating to expenses in respect of qualifying and appeal proceedings but it is important, particularly when the rules of court are not yet in force, that the expenses incurred when drafting and negotiating the agreement are included at the time of settlement.

The only caveat is the backdrop of section 8 of the Litigation (Expenses and Group Proceedings) (Scotland) Act 2018, which is now in force. Qualified one way costs shifting applies to personal injury actions but the conduct of the pursuer and their agents is always a relevant consideration when expenses are being determined by court.

The question does arise as to whether the defenders will be able to lodge tenders in respect of the periodical payment order and whether similarly, pursuers will be able to lodge pursuers offers in a similar manner.

It remains to be seen the form in which tenders will be lodged and their effectiveness in cases where periodical payment orders are being sought or applied by court. Currently, as a periodical payment order cannot be granted by court unilaterally, it is not competent to tender in respect of a periodical payment orders terms. Presently, a tender can only be lodged in the form of a traditional lump sum offer. The rules of court that will be issued may provide further clarity on the manner in which to do this but likely a body of authority will develop over time once the legislation is fully in force.

The difficulty with tenders or pursuer's offers in this situation will arise insofar as effectively advising clients on the prospects of beating them in court. The court would have to look at the lump sum offered;

the nature of annual payments for each head of claim; the index used and the frequency of payments in the round before making a decision on whether a party has beaten the tender or not. This assessment will likely differ depending on the judge deciding on the case this leads to uncertainty in advice. The task itself for the presiding judge will also be difficult as there would be so many factors to consider rather than simply whether a traditional lump sum award had been between on not.

The terms of a periodical payment order are complex and it is anticipated that being able to give advice on whether a client either has or will beat a tender will be almost impossible. Certainty of legal advice is very important particularly when acting for vulnerable clients. The difficulties in providing advice in respect of tenders will in turn cause issues where clients have taken out after the even insurance to fund their cases. There is an obligation to provide advice on tenders to both the client and funders of the case, which could cause difficulties with funding. It remains to be seen what the rules will say in this regard but it might be sensible for some time to pass and see how periodical payment orders are applied before the ability to tender is permitted. Expenses are always at the discretion of the court and it may be that expenses should be looked at in the round at the conclusion of the case.

A further difficulty may arise where a tender is only lodged in the form of settlement that that defender prefers. This could put pressure on vulnerable pursuers. Much will depend on what the rules of court say but one can imagine the situation where the clear preference of the defender is settlement by means of a periodical payment order and a tender is lodged for settlement in this manner. It would be sensible to also lodge a tender for the traditional lump sum award but it could be at a lower sum than the periodical payment order tender. This may not offer much protection for the defenders but could put the pursuer in a difficult situation if they do not wish to proceed to court.

As the rules of court are not yet in force, there is no provision at present for recovery of fees associated with the drafting and negotiation of the agreement itself if settlement is agreed using the Court of Session scale of expenses. It is therefore important that there is a contractual agreement between parties regarding the recovery of the expenses occasioned by the drafting and negotiation of the periodical payment order agreement. Significant time will be incurred by both agents and counsel and professional input will be required. Additional outlays will therefore be incurred over and above the usual court process.

As mentioned previously, it is important that the IFA and actuary are certified as experts to allow recovery of their report outlays and their attendance at the pre-trial meeting (if that took place) as part of the account of expenses.

Settling a case by means of a periodical payment order (or obtaining an award from court) also gives agents further grounds to pursue a motion for additional fee. It is likely that an additional fee would be sought in any event in these sorts of cases but settling by means of this order increases the complexity element of the case and is indeed novel as comparably few cases have settled to date by means of a periodical payment order. It allows these cases to stand apart from other serious injury cases.

It remains to be seen what the rules of court will make provision for in terms of expenses but it is important that if a periodical payment order is being agreed prior to the legislation coming into force that agents agree that expenses incurred dealing with the agreement itself are part of settlement terms. This, in practice, is not included in the joint minute itself as it is not competent but instead is agreed contractually between parties.

CHAPTER TWELVE

CONCLUSION

The Act has certainly provided the backdrop for a brave new world in serious injury cases in Scotland. It remains to be seen when the rules of court will be published allowing for implementation of part 2 of the Act and what the terms of the rules will be. The approach adopted in England and Wales is likely to be looked at with interest by practitioners in Scotland. A significant body of authority has built up and lessons seem to have been learned in the application of periodical payment orders over the years. It seems wasteful for Scotland not to benefit from their experiences but the use of periodical payment orders must be looked at in the context of pursuing claims in Scotland.

There certainly should be an appetite for the use of periodical payment orders by practitioners in cases of more substantial value due to many of the advantages that they hold. However, hopefully this book has demonstrated that significant amounts of work needs to be done by agents when the use of a periodical payment order is even being considered and to get to the stage of deciding upon whether this mode of settlement would suit the needs of the client. A periodical payment order may not be suitable when the individual circumstances of the case are considered in detail.

It is very much a balancing act that needs to be carried out, putting the interests of the injured party, their needs and their preferences at the centre of decision making. Proper financial advice should underpin the decision-making process but ultimately, if a pursuer walks into a court room, they must be aware of the risk that the court may take this decision out of their hands if it deems it to be in the best interests of the pursuer. The caveat is that the court should always take the pursuer's needs and preference into consideration under the Act.

This will become an added risk factor when proceeding to proof in any serious injury case and proper advice must be given to clients to ensure that any decisions taken in relation to their case are fully informed.

It remains to be seen how the legislation in Scotland will be implemented but there is an attraction to the use of periodical payment orders in suitable cases and likely they will become much more prevalent in the future. Practitioners wait in anticipation to see what the future holds but the landscape is changing and we must be ready for what is to come.

MORE BOOKS BY LAW BRIEF PUBLISHING

'Covid-19, Homeworking and the Law – The Essential Guide to Employment and GDPR Issues' by Forbes Solicitors
'Covid-19, Force Majeure and Frustration of Contracts – The Essential Guide' by Keith Markham
'Covid-19 and Criminal Law – The Essential Guide' by Ramya Nagesh
'Covid-19 and Family Law in England and Wales – The Essential Guide' by Safda Mahmood
'A Practical Guide to the Law of Unlawful Eviction and Harassment – 2nd Edition' by Stephanie Lovegrove
'Covid-19, Residential Property, Equity Release and Enfranchisement – The Essential Guide' by Paul Sams and Louise Uphill
'Covid-19, Brexit and the Law of Commercial Leases – The Essential Guide' by Mark Shelton
'A Practical Guide to Costs in Personal Injury Claims – 2nd Edition' by Matthew Hoe
'A Practical Guide to the General Data Protection Regulation (GDPR) – 2nd Edition' by Keith Markham
'Ellis on Credit Hire – Sixth Edition' by Aidan Ellis & Tim Kevan
'A Practical Guide to Working with Litigants in Person and McKenzie Friends in Family Cases' by Stuart Barlow
'Protecting Unregistered Brands: A Practical Guide to the Law of Passing Off' by Lorna Brazell
'A Practical Guide to Secondary Liability and Joint Enterprise Post-Jogee' by Joanne Cecil & James Mehigan
'A Practical Guide to the Pre-Action RTA Claims Protocol for Personal Injury Lawyers' by Antonia Ford
'A Practical Guide to Neighbour Disputes and the Law' by Alexander Walsh
'A Practical Guide to Forfeiture of Leases' by Mark Shelton
'A Practical Guide to Coercive Control for Legal Practitioners and Victims' by Rachel Horman

'A Practical Guide to Rights Over Airspace and Subsoil' by Daniel Gatty
'Tackling Disclosure in the Criminal Courts – A Practitioner's Guide' by Narita Bahra QC & Don Ramble
'A Practical Guide to the Law of Driverless Cars – Second Edition' by Alex Glassbrook, Emma Northey & Scarlett Milligan
'A Practical Guide to TOLATA Claims' by Greg Williams
'Artificial Intelligence – The Practical Legal Issues' by John Buyers
'A Practical Guide to the Law of Prescription in Scotland' by Andrew Foyle
'A Practical Guide to the Construction and Rectification of Wills and Trust Instruments' by Edward Hewitt
'A Practical Guide to the Law of Bullying and Harassment in the Workplace' by Philip Hyland
'How to Be a Freelance Solicitor: A Practical Guide to the SRA-Regulated Freelance Solicitor Model' by Paul Bennett
'A Practical Guide to Prison Injury Claims' by Malcolm Johnson
'A Practical Guide to the Small Claims Track' by Dominic Bright
'A Practical Guide to Advising Clients at the Police Station' by Colin Stephen McKeown-Beaumont
'A Practical Guide to Antisocial Behaviour Injunctions' by Iain Wightwick
'Practical Mediation: A Guide for Mediators, Advocates, Advisers, Lawyers, and Students in Civil, Commercial, Business, Property, Workplace, and Employment Cases' by Jonathan Dingle with John Sephton
'The Mini-Pupillage Workbook' by David Boyle
'A Practical Guide to Crofting Law' by Brian Inkster
'A Practical Guide to Spousal Maintenance' by Liz Cowell
'A Practical Guide to the Law of Domain Names and Cybersquatting' by Andrew Clemson
'A Practical Guide to the Law of Gender Pay Gap Reporting' by Harini Iyengar

'A Practical Guide to the Rights of Grandparents in Children Proceedings' by Stuart Barlow
'NHS Whistleblowing and the Law' by Joseph England
'Employment Law and the Gig Economy' by Nigel Mackay & Annie Powell
'A Practical Guide to Noise Induced Hearing Loss (NIHL) Claims' by Andrew Mckie, Ian Skeate, Gareth McAloon
'An Introduction to Beauty Negligence Claims – A Practical Guide for the Personal Injury Practitioner' by Greg Almond
'Intercompany Agreements for Transfer Pricing Compliance' by Paul Sutton
'Zen and the Art of Mediation' by Martin Plowman
'A Practical Guide to the SRA Principles, Individual and Law Firm Codes of Conduct 2019 – What Every Law Firm Needs to Know' by Paul Bennett
'A Practical Guide to Adoption for Family Lawyers' by Graham Pegg
'A Practical Guide to Industrial Disease Claims' by Andrew Mckie & Ian Skeate
'A Practical Guide to Redundancy' by Philip Hyland
'A Practical Guide to Vicarious Liability' by Mariel Irvine
'A Practical Guide to Applications for Landlord's Consent and Variation of Leases' by Mark Shelton
'A Practical Guide to Relief from Sanctions Post-Mitchell and Denton' by Peter Causton
'A Practical Guide to Equity Release for Advisors' by Paul Sams
'A Practical Guide to the Law Relating to Food' by Ian Thomas
'A Practical Guide to Financial Services Claims' by Chris Hegarty
'The Law of Houses in Multiple Occupation: A Practical Guide to HMO Proceedings' by Julian Hunt
'A Practical Guide to Unlawful Eviction and Harassment' by Stephanie Lovegrove
'Occupiers, Highways and Defective Premises Claims: A Practical Guide Post-Jackson – 2nd Edition' by Andrew Mckie

www.ingramcontent.com/pod-product-compliance
Ingram Content Group UK Ltd.
Pitfield, Milton Keynes, MK11 3LW, UK
UKHW020151290926
15471UKWH00004B/805

9 781914 608155